ANIMAL SENSES

JODIE MANGOR

ROURKE
Educational Media

rourkeeducationalmedia.com

Before & After Reading Activities

Teaching Focus:

Have students locate the ending punctuation for sentences in the book. Count how many times a period, question mark, or exclamation point is used. Which one is used the most? What is the purpose for each ending punctuation mark? Practice reading these sentences with appropriate expression.

Before Reading:

Building Academic Vocabulary and Background Knowledge

Before reading a book, it is important to set the stage for your child or student by using pre-reading strategies. This will help them develop their vocabulary, increase their reading comprehension, and make connections across the curriculum.

1. Look at the cover of the book. What will this book be about?
2. What do you already know about the topic?
3. Let's study the Table of Contents. What will you learn about in the book's chapters?
4. What would you like to learn about this topic? Do you think you might learn about it from this book? Why or why not?
5. Use a reading journal to write about your knowledge of this topic. Record what you already know about the topic and what you hope to learn about the topic.
6. Read the book.
7. In your reading journal, record what you learned about the topic and your response to the book.
8. After reading the book complete the activities below.

Content Area Vocabulary

Read the list. What do these words mean?

cells
detect
echolocation
environment
interprets
mates
organs
prey
receptors
tentacles

After Reading:

Comprehension and Extension Activity

After reading the book, work on the following questions with your child or students to check their level of reading comprehension and content mastery.

1. What do animals use their senses for? (Summarize)
2. How does an animal's habitat affect its senses? (Infer)
3. What is an example of an animal sense that people don't have? (Asking Questions)
4. How do your senses compare to a bear's? (Text to Self Connection)
5. How can an animal's eyes and ears help us to figure out if they are a predator or prey? (Asking Questions)

Extension Activity

Pick an animal that you are interested in and research its senses. Which sense does it rely on the most? The least? How do its senses compare to yours? Draw a diagram of the animal, labeling each of its senses and what it uses them for.

TABLE OF CONTENTS

SENSING THE WORLD

Animals have senses to help them survive. Like humans, most animals can touch, taste, see, smell, and hear. Animals use their senses to find food, water, and shelter. They also use them to find each other, protect themselves, and escape danger.

Each sense is connected to one or more body parts called **organs**. Eyes, noses, tongues, skin, and ears are all sense organs. These organs collect information about an animal's **environment** and send it to the brain.

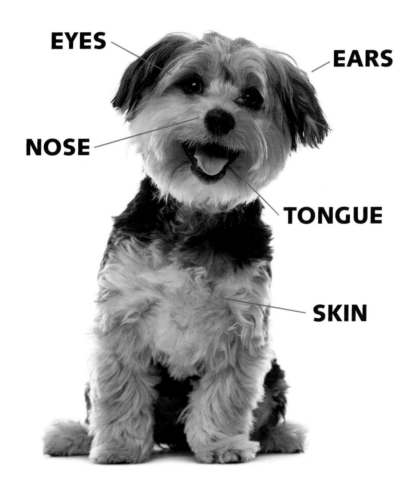

EYES

EARS

NOSE

TONGUE

SKIN

Animals live in a variety of habitats. Each type of animal has developed senses that help it survive in its particular habitat.

Get a Clue!

There are many types of ears, eyes, tongues, noses, whiskers and skin. These body parts give us clues about how an animal lives.

For example, a desert snake can sense its **prey,** a kangaroo rat, in the dark. But the kangaroo rat can hear the snake sliding toward it over the sand. Both are using their senses to help them survive.

Animals with large ears usually have excellent hearing.

SIGHT

Many animals rely on their sense of sight to get around. Some animals see fewer colors than humans. Some see more. Scientists think birds and butterflies might see 1,000 times more colors than humans!

Chameleons can move each of their eyes separately.

Scientists discovered that reindeer can see ultraviolet light. This makes some things, like the lichen they eat, look dark against the snow. It also helps the reindeer spot light-colored wolves from a long way off. Other Arctic mammals may also share this ability.

Human Vision

Bee Vision

Birds, butterflies, and bees can see patterns on flowers that human eyes cannot.

Invisible Light

The colors we see come from waves of light. Ultraviolet (UV) light has wavelengths that are shorter than visible light. These waves are invisible to the human eye.

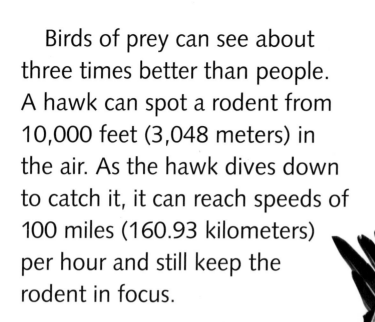

Birds of prey can see about three times better than people. A hawk can spot a rodent from 10,000 feet (3,048 meters) in the air. As the hawk dives down to catch it, it can reach speeds of 100 miles (160.93 kilometers) per hour and still keep the rodent in focus.

*There's a saying:
"Eyes on the side,
born to hide;
eyes on the front,
born to hunt."*

Eye See You

Hunters' eyes often face forward to target their prey. Prey animals usually have eyes on the sides of their head to see all around to watch for danger.

Animals that are active at night, such as cats, owls, and geckos, have eyes designed to see well in the dark. Their eyes are often large and have pupils that can get very wide. Inside their eyes, a special layer of **cells** acts like a mirror. These features help collect more light.

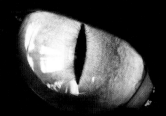

Many nocturnal animals have pupils that close to form slits in the daylight.

SMELL AND TASTE

Smell and taste are important senses for finding food. Animals also use smell to locate **mates** and offspring, avoid enemies, and mark their territory. Taste can help an animal tell if something is poisonous.

A dog's sense of smell is 10,000 times more sensitive than a human's. A bear's sense of smell is even better. Black bears can smell food up to 18 miles (28.97 kilometers) away. Polar bears can smell a seal through 3 feet (1 meter) of snow.

Bears have much smaller brains than humans. But a much bigger area of a bear's brain is used for smell.

Smelling in Stereo
A rat's nostrils can work independently of each other. This allows the rat to figure out the direction a smell is coming from.

Most animals taste with their tongues. A tongue is covered with nerves, or taste buds. These send messages to the brain. The brain **interprets** the taste.

Tasty Toes

Butterflies taste with sense organs located on their feet. When they land, they immediately know if they're on something good to eat.

Humans have about 10,000 taste buds. Cats have about 500 taste buds. Chickens have just 24. Cows, on the other hand, have about 25,000. Their sense of taste helps them decide which plants are safe to eat.

Catfish can **detect** tiny amounts of food in dark, cloudy water. They have as many as 250,000 taste **receptors** spread over the surface of their bodies. Most are on the whiskers, also called barbels, around their mouth.

LET'S EXPERIMENT!

A dog needs to have a wet tongue to taste. Is this true for humans?

To find out, you'll need:

1. A pinch of salt and a pinch of sugar, mixed together
2. Optional: other dry foods (crackers, cereal, powdered milk, etc.)
3. A glass of water
4. Paper towel

What to do:

1. First, you'll need to dry off your tongue. You can do this by sticking your tongue out and panting or drying your tongue off with a paper towel.
2. Without putting your tongue back into your mouth, sprinkle the salt and sugar mixture onto your tongue.
3. Wait 5 seconds—can you taste anything?
4. Now bring your tongue back inside your mouth and let your saliva wash over it. How does this affect your ability to taste?
5. Sip some water to cleanse your mouth and repeat with other dry foods.

What's Happening?

Our taste buds convert some of the chemicals in food into electric signals that travel to the brain. They need liquid to do this.

TOUCH

An animal's sense of touch can help it find food and shelter. Touch can also help it move around in the dark.

Star-nosed moles spend almost all their time underground. Their nose **tentacles** have six times more touch receptors than a person's hand. These sensitive tentacles help them find their way.

Crocodiles have about 9,000 sensors around their heads, jaws, and bodies. The sensors can detect even the tiniest ripple in the water. They help crocodiles hunt prey.

Manatees have special hairs all over their bodies.
These hairs can detect changes in water movement
and temperature.

Wondrous Whiskers

Many mammals have whiskers. A cat's
whiskers are very sensitive. They help it
judge size and distance and feel slight
shifts in the air.

LET'S EXPERIMENT!

How sensitive is your sense of touch? To find out, you'll need:

1. 5 different grades of sandpaper
2. Scissors
3. A marker
4. A blindfold

What to do:

1. Cut an index card-sized rectangle from the roughest grade of sandpaper. Using a marker, write "1" on the back.
2. Do the same for the second roughest grade, this time labeling the piece with a "2."
3. Do the same thing for the remaining three grades of sandpaper, labeling the pieces "3", "4", and "5", from rough to smooth.
4. Now put on a blindfold.
5. Mix up the pieces and turn them all rough side up.
6. Using your sense of touch, try to order the pieces from roughest to smoothest.
7. Take off your blindfold.
8. Flip over the pieces of sandpaper. Are their numbers ordered 1 to 5?
9. If this was easy, try a matching game: make a second set of sandpaper rectangles just like the first. Mix all 10 cards together, put on your blindfold and try to match up identical pairs.

Our fingertips have a strong sense of touch. But our sense of touch can become less sensitive when it is exposed to something for a long time. This is why we barely notice our clothes, glasses, or jewelry after wearing them for a while. Do you think this is an advantage or disadvantage?

HEARING

Animals use their hearing for many things: to sense danger, prey, and other animals. Humans only hear some of the sounds around us. Some animals, like mice, can hear in a higher range. Elephants and pigeons can detect sounds that are too low for people to hear.

Elephants use their ears, trunks, and feet to detect sounds 20 times lower than humans can hear. Elephants can send each other low-frequency messages. These can travel over long distances, as far as 3.7 miles (6 kilometers).

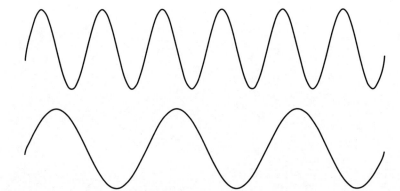

High Pitch

Low Pitch

Fun Fact

Black grouse use low sounds to call to mates through dense forests. These birds can also hear the low rumble of a faraway thunderstorm.

An owl uses its hearing to find prey in the dark. One ear is set higher on the head than the other. This helps the owl know where a quiet sound, like a mouse rustling in the leaves, is coming from.

Prey animals such as rabbits and deer often have large ears that can move around. Their ears help them hear sounds from every direction.

Listen Up!

Like eyes, the direction an animal's ears face can tell us if that animal is prey or a predator. Predators have forward-facing ears. Prey animals have side-facing ears.

SPECIAL SENSES

Some animals have developed senses that humans don't have.

Sharks, platypuses, and some fish can sense the electric fields of other animals in the water. Some birds can sense Earth's magnetic field. They use it to find their way when migrating.

Most bats, whales, and dolphins use sound to track prey. First, they make a sound. The echo that bounces back gives them information about their surroundings. This is called **echolocation.**

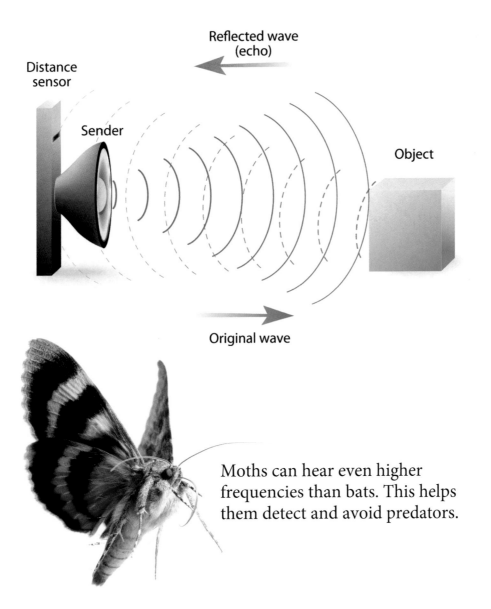

Reflected wave (echo)

Distance sensor

Sender

Object

Original wave

Moths can hear even higher frequencies than bats. This helps them detect and avoid predators.

Vampire bats drink the blood of other animals. They find their prey using a patch of skin on their face called a nose leaf. This organ can sense heat from another animal, and even help the bat zero in on a vein.

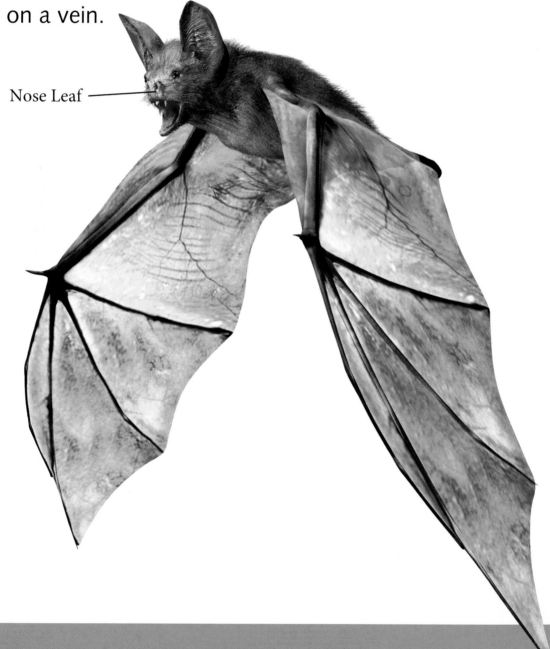

Nose Leaf

A blind cave fish can't see. It finds food using its lateral line organ. Many fish have this type of organ. It detects changes in water pressure. This allows the fish to feel nearby movements in the water.

Superior Senses

Compared to humans, many animals have amazing senses. Technologies such as virtual reality may give us the chance to experience the world through the senses of different animals.

GLOSSARY

cells (selz): the smallest units of an animal or a plant

detect (di-TEKT): to notice or discover something

echolocation (EK-oh-loh-KAY-shuhn): the ability to locate faraway objects by sending sound waves and sensing them as they bounce off the object

environment (en-VYE-ruhn-muhnt): the natural surroundings of living things, such as the air, land, or sea

interprets (in-TUR-prits): figures out what something means

mates (mates): the male or female partners of animals

organs (OR-guhns): parts of the body, such as the heart or the kidneys, that have a certain purpose

prey (pray): an animal that is hunted by another animal for food

receptors (ri-SEP-tors): nerves that detect a particular chemical or force

tentacles (TEN-tuh-kuhls): the long, flexible limbs of some animals such as jellyfish, octopuses, squid and sea anemones

INDEX

SHOW WHAT YOU KNOW

1. List some of the ways animals use their senses to survive.

2. Why do animals develop certain types of senses?

3. How do taste buds work?

4. What are some of the ways animals use their sense of touch?

5. Name a sense that some animals have, but people don't.

WEBSITES TO VISIT

www.faculty.washington.edu/chudler/amaze.html

www.kids.nationalgeographic.com/animals

www.sciencenewsforstudents.org/article/sense-danger

ABOUT THE AUTHOR

Jodie Mangor writes magazine articles and books for children. She is also the author of audio tour scripts for high-profile museums and tourist destinations around the world. Many of these tours are for kids. She lives in Ithaca, New York, together with Mishka the dog, Olaf the crested gecko, Pippo the cat, and her family.

Meet The Author!
www.meetREMauthors.com

© 2018 Rourke Educational Media

www.rourkeeducationalmedia.com

PHOTO CREDITS: Cover and title page: ©animalnige; table of contents: ©Andrea Izzotti; p.4: ©UrosPoteko; p.5, 10: ©GlobalIP; p.6: ©Oktay Ortakcioglu; p.7: ©YasserBadr.Bennthere; p.8: ©Milan Lipowski; p.9: ©Dr Schmitt, Weinheim Germany, ©arlindo71; p.10: ©Steve Mcsweeny; p.11: ©Ekaterina Shvigert; p.12: ©nicholas belton; p.13: ©David Yang, ©MikeSPb; p.14: ©purple_queue, ©KirsanovV; p.15: ©LPETTET; p.16: ©abadonian; p.18: ©Dieter Meyrl; p.19: ©Carlos Alvarez; p.20: ©fmajor, ©shaunl; p.22: ©Johan Swanepoel; p.23: ©MikeLane45; p.24: ©Vasiliki Varvaki; p.25: ©Voren1; p.26: ©RamonCarretero; p.27: ©ttsz, ©Antagain; p.28: ©Geerati; p.29: Public Doman, ©Daniel Chetroni

Edited by: Keli Sipperley
Cover design by: Rhea Magaro-Wallace
Interior design by: Kathy Walsh

Library of Congress PCN Data

Animal Senses / Jodie Mangor
(Science Alliance)
 ISBN 978-1-68342-350-8 (hard cover)
 ISBN 978-1-68342-446-8 (soft cover)
 ISBN 978-1-68342-516-8 (e-Book)
Library of Congress Control Number: 2017931194

Rourke Educational Media
Printed in the United States of America,
North Mankato, Minnesota